The Living World of Audubon

The Living World of AUDU

designed by Albert Squillace

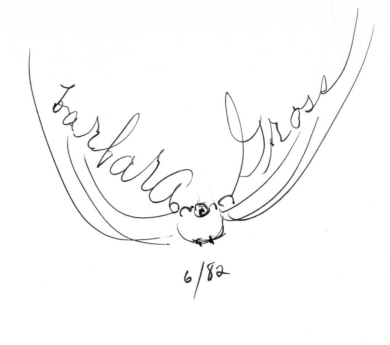

barbara Gross

6/82

FIRESIDE

JBON

by Roland C. Clement
Vice President of the National Audubon Society

A Fireside Book / Published by Simon and Schuster, New York

Prepared and Produced by The Ridge Press, Inc.
Hardcover edition published in 1974 by Grosset & Dunlap, Inc.

A Fireside Book Trade Paperback published in 1980 by Simon & Schuster.
A Division of Gulf & Western Corporation
Simon & Schuster Building
Rockfeller Center
1230 Avenue of the Americas
New York, New York 10020
FIRESIDE and colophon are trademarks of Simon & Schuster
Library of Congress Catalog Card Number: 80-52492
ISBN: 0-671-41881-5

Printed in the United States of America by Rand McNally & Company

To Muriel

Contents

Introduction

Although another book on John James Audubon may seem to deny the claim, it
is time to insist that we have had too much of the cult of genius, of the singular
individual who, we falsely imagine, can sense things none of the rest
of us can glimpse. This attitude (much to the fore in the last century) has
almost alienated the artist by making him seem and feel eccentric.
Most people tend to experience the world in terms of the trappings that stand for it,
and it may be that anyone who insists—as the artist must—on addressing the
real world is, almost by definition, eccentric. Society suffers
in consequence of this mistaken emphasis on the artist as a being apart, for
we need the artist as part of our workaday world—today more than ever—to help
us surmount the shallow outlook fostered by commerce.

What is singular about Audubon the artist is the strength of his
initiative in exploring and expressing nature by focusing on birds as examples
of the life process. Most of us look without seeing. Audubon's
greatness is that he excelled—as one self-trained—in seeing and expressing the
reality which, though present to all of us, goes largely unseen. It is
literally true that the artist paints in order to see
better, and thereby he becomes a pathfinder.

If this view of art and the artist's role is sound, it must
follow that the scientist, too—as ornithologist, ethologist, ecologist—has new
things to tell us about birds and all reality. Art, science,
philosophy—all human striving at expression—are methodologies in the endless
quest for understanding of an ever larger reality.

The artist's contribution to ecology is obvious—though
seldom explicitly acknowledged by ecologists, because ecologists, like all of
us, suffer from an excess of individualism. We see this ecological
contribution in the teachings of the great English landscapist, Joseph Turner, who
more than a century ago focused on portraying the significance of
light in the landscape. Turner, who studied nature even more intently than
Audubon and at about the same time, insisted that "every look at

nature is a refinement upon art. Each tree and blade of grass or flower is
not to him (the artist) the indiviudal tree, grass or flower,
but what it is in relation to the whole, its tone, its contrast and its use."
The artist, he saw, admires nature by the power of his art,
always a limited power because each of us is bolstered and limited by his time;
and he judges his art by new perceptions drawn from nature.
Turner and Audubon were both pioneers in that exciting era when, under their
tutelage and that of men like Darwin, Humboldt, Agassiz, Thoreau, and Cézanne,
the Western World was learning to see its environment in a new way.
Both men died in 1851.

We are again on the verge of learning to see our world anew, this
time through the insights of ecology. The great increase of ornithological
art in our day is a sure indication of the broadening of environmental
awareness. A generation ago there were hardly six men whose
work was worthy of attention; today there are at least a score, and their
number grows apace. This reflects the willingness of the times to
support them, though not as well as many deserve.

Every new advance begins by emphasizing the neglected insights
of the prior wave of explorers. The ground needs reworking. Not even Darwin's
hundred-year-old insights have yet been made part of
the awareness of the average man. The need to refocus attention on a very
few great producers of yesteryear reflects the still
backward state of public awareness. If it were otherwise, if the public were ready
to receive the artistic and ecological insights of contemporary
workers in the nature field, publishers would certainly take note. As it is,
modern ornithological painters still lack a large audience and
the means of publication and are thus discouraged from gaining new insights
from nature and articulating them for our joint benefit. This is why
art should not be thought of as a luxury, and why each of us should participate
in artistic production wherever our talents suggest it.
We must view art not as the production of "works of art," but as serious self-expression

in every field of endeavor. Life itself is art, if we savor it at all.

As a small contribution to keeping art's search for
truth alive, and to show how truly exciting birds can be, we have gone back to
some of Audubon's most vibrant plates.
The painter seeks to capture that
single pose, or those few poses that are balanced enough to convey the grace of a live bird.
Not all the artist's attempts to capture
the beauty of birds are equally successful. But when to a good likeness is added some
essence of the dynamic tensions involved in life itself, we
recognize this and call it art.

Audubon's great work, *Birds of America,* pictured 435 species, the larger
birds done in the field and in his studio while he lived in America. But many of
the smaller birds were done in England, after 1826, while he was
seeing to the publication of the work.

An original Audubon print is an engraving that has been hand-
colored. Audubon made his original paintings in watercolor and oil, then had engravings
made on copper plates, first by Lizars of Edinburgh, Scotland,
then by Havell of London. The large size selected is called a double elephant folio
in the publishing trade. Bound volumes of these extraordinary
prints originally were sold for about $1,000 per set. In 1969, one set (plus a few)
extra prints) sold for more than $200,000.

While seeing to the engraving and hand-coloring, and doing his own
selling of sets, Audubon also wrote a five-volume *Ornithological Biography,* which
provides an anecdotal account of his studies of American birds.
A fascinating account of the production of the *Birds of America* is told in
a scholarly book, *The Double Elephant Folio* by Waldemar H. Fries, which was published by the
American Library Association in 1973.

Author and publisher owe special thanks to Nancy
Manson, Librarian of the National Audubon Society, to Sam Dasher, of the
Society's Photo and Film Department, and to Vincent Brenwasser,
who photographed the Audubon folios for this book.

306
Common Loon
Gavia immer

How do Audubon's birds fare today?
A few have increased in number and even extended their
ranges, but many others—like the loon—have
decreased both in numbers
and distribution. The "great northern diver" is still
a common bird in appropriate places.
In Audubon's day it nested as far south as the Wabash
and Susquehanna; today only some
of the northern-tier United States and parts of Canada
know it as a nesting bird. With the coming of winter,
it leaves the northern lakes and heads for the large bays
and the coastal seas, where—singly or in small groups—
it fishes and awaits the coming of another
spring. "Whether it be fishing in deep
water amid rolling billows," Audubon wrote,
"or engaged in eluding its foes, it disappears
beneath the surface so suddenly, remains so long
in the water, and rises at so extraordinary a distance,
often in a direction quite the reverse of that
supposed to be followed by it, that
your eyes become wearied in searching for it."

311
White Pelican
Pelecanus erythrorhynchos

Audubon was unlucky in observing this great
bird. He was the first field
naturalist to distinguish our American White Pelican
from the somewhat similar Eurasian
bird, only to have his proudly bestowed name, *Americanus*,
pre-empted by the fact that the
eighteenth-century ornithologist, Gmelin, who never saw the
bird alive, had already given it a
scientific moniker based on specimen materials shipped to him
in Europe. And Audubon never saw the large
ground-nesting colonies that are now much more sparsely scattered
across interior and western North America, because
his Texas visit did not penetrate quite far enough—to the
latitude of Corpus Christi, where the only
Gulf Coast colony persists to this day. Thanks, probably,
to a different physiology and to
somewhat different feeding habits, this big white
fish-eater was not affected by chemical
pesticides as was the Brown Pelican. We are thereby
reminded that every species is
indeed unique; nay, every individual is unique,
since each of us is a very
special "print-out" of a long evolutionary
history which culminates in us.

251

Brown Pelican
Pelecanus occidentalis

"I doubt . . . if I ever felt greater pleasure than I
do at this moment, when, with my journal at my side, and the gulls
and pelicans in my mind's eye as distinctly as I could
wish, I ponder on the faculties which Nature has bestowed on animals which
we merely consider as possessed of instinct." The event Audubon
was commenting upon in this passage is an earlier
description of an interesting association wherein Laughing Gulls
often help themselves to fish escaping the pelican's big bill as it surfaces
after a successful dive. The pelican's fishing dives are spectacular
maneuvers in which it may plunge from heights of fifteen to twenty
feet. Although pushed back by man's occupancy of so much of North America's
coastal lands, the Brown Pelican held its own until the
mid-fifties, when its population collapsed because of environmental
poisoning by chemical pesticides. Fortunately,
timely restrictions on the use of these poisons have
promoted a slow comeback of pelicans and other fish-eating birds.

326
Gannet
Morus bassanus

"On the morning of the 14th of June, 1833, the white sails of the
Ripley were spread before a propitious breeze, and onward she might be seen
gaily wending her way toward the shores of Labrador. As we approached
[the Great Gannet Rock in the Gulf of St. Lawrence], I imagined that the atmosphere
around was filled with flakes, but on my turning to the pilot,
who smiled at my simplicity, I was assured that nothing was in sight but the
Gannets and their island home. I rubbed my eyes, took up my glass,
and saw that the strange dimness of the air before us was caused by the innumerable
birds, whose white bodies and black-tipped pinions produced a blended
tint of grey. When we had advanced to within half a mile, this magnificent veil
of floating Gannets was easily seen, now shooting upwards, as if
intent on reaching the sky, then descending as if to join the feathered masses
below, and again diverging toward either side and sweeping over
the surface of the ocean." Today one goes to Bonaventure Island, off the
tip of the Gaspé Peninsula in Quebec, to enjoy Gannets.

211

Great Blue Heron
Ardea herodias

Audubon's imaginativeness in fitting even
the largest birds to the dimensions of his folio sheets
is well illustrated by his painting of the
Great Blue Heron and that of the American Flamingo. No one before
him dared such contortions, so great a departure from
convention, yet the result is dynamic rather than grotesque.
"The flight of the Great Blue Heron," Audubon wrote,
"is even, powerful, and capable of being protracted to a great
distance. On rising from the ground or on leaving
its perch, it goes off in silence with extended neck and dangling legs,
for eight or ten yards, after which it draws back its neck,
extends its feet in a straight line behind, and with easy
and measured flappings continues its course, at times flying low over
the marshes, and again, as if suspecting danger,
at a considerable height over the land or the forest." Like
most herons, these nest colonially in suitable places
across the country, usually on small islands or in tall trees
bordering marshy areas. The Great White Heron of
Florida Bay has recently been labeled a mere color form (morph)
of the Great Blue Heron. The term "Blue Crane"
is, of course, a misnomer for this bird.

PLATE

333
Green Heron
Butorides virescens

Still a widespread bird, the
Green Heron is nevertheless probably much less
numerous than it was in Audubon's day,
when mill ponds and small wetlands dotted the landscape
much more extensively than they do today.
We have probably lost much of the intimacy of these birds also.
Audubon wrote: "It is little alarmed by the presence
of man, and you may often see it close to houses
on the mill-dams, or even raising its brood on the trees
of gardens. The gentleness, or as many would say,
the stupidity of the bird is truly remarkable, for it
will at times allow you to approach within a few
paces, looking as unconcernedly upon you as the
House Sparrow is wont to do in the streets of London."
The name Green Heron is at first puzzling
because this bird appears slate-blue most of the time.
It is only in strong light or in the hand
that the green sheen of its plumage is appreciated.
The bright orange legs are distinctive
at almost any distance. Small herons of this type occur
throughout the world, except in western Eurasia.

PLATE CCC

242

Snowy Egret
Leucophoyx thula

An egret is a heron, but the name is
usually restricted to those white herons that carry a
spray of curved nuptial plumes on their back
during the breeding season. At the turn of the
century, these plumes, which the French called aigrettes,
were seen everywhere on women's hats. Audubon
considered them especially gentle birds and wrote:
"At the approach of the breeding season, many
spend a great part of the day at their roosting places,
perched on the low trees principally growing
in the water, when every now and then they utter a rough
guttural sort of sigh, raising at the same moment
their beautiful crest and loose recurved
plumes, curving the neck, and rising on their legs to their
full height, as if about to strut on the branches.
They act in the same manner while on the ground mating.
Then the male, with great ardor, and with
the most graceful motions, passes and repasses for several
minutes at a time before and around the female,
whose actions are similar, although she displays less
ardor." Although still widespread, the Snowy
Egret is much less numerous than
it was in Audubon's day.

236
Black-crowned Night Heron
Nycticorax nycticorax

"On the ground," Audubon wrote,
"this bird exhibits none of the grace observed
in all the true herons; it walks in a
stooping posture, the neck much retracted, until
it sees its prey, when, with a sudden
movement, it stretches it out and secures its food.
It is never seen standing motionless,
waiting for its prey, like the true herons, but
is constantly moving about in search of it.
Its feeding places are the sides of ditches, meadows,
the shady banks of creeks, bayous, and
ponds or rivers, as well as the extensive salt marshes
and mud-bars left exposed at low water.
When satisfied, it retires to some high tree on
the banks of a stream or in the interior of a swamp, and
there it stands, usually on one leg, for
hours at a time, apparently dosing, though seldom sound
asleep." He also called it Qua-Bird, from the loud
call which gives it the onomatopoeic name of
Quawk in most of New England. These chunky, nearly
cosmopolitan night herons move from feeding to roosting
areas during the twilight hours. They nest
colonially, ten to a hundred pairs or more together,
in wooded thickets near or over the water.

431

American Flamingo
Phoenicopterus ruber

"Far away to the seaward we spied a
flock of flamingoes advancing in 'Indian line'
with well-spread wings, outstretched necks, and long legs
directed backwards. Ah! reader, could you but know the emotions
that then agitated my breast! I thought I had
now reached the height of all my expectations, for my voyage to the
Floridas was undertaken in a great measure for the
purpose of studying these lovely birds in their own beautiful
islands." Gregarious in nature, flamingos sometimes
mass in huge numbers, at which time they indeed constitute one
of the most spectacular sights of the bird world—
perhaps even of the animal world—when one considers their bright
colors, their extraordinarily exaggerated proportions,
and their flight. Our American flamingo, a Caribbean bird principally,
is the world's most colorful, though other species occur in
the saline ponds of other tropical areas, sometimes—as in South
America's Andes—at high altitude. The extraordinary bill
of the flamingo houses a filter-feeding mechanism
very reminiscent of the baleen whale's.

201

Canada Goose

Branta canadensis

In his writing on this great bird,

Audubon reveals what an avid hunter he was.

He took birds for food, for study—even for what may seem

the casual satisfaction of his abiding curiosity—and, of course, to serve as

models for his paintings. Many today belittle him for

this robust interest, pursued (it now seems) immoderately. Yet how can one

judge another apart from his circumstances? Audubon

lived when our continent was much richer in resources—when, indeed, most

people thought those resources absolutely unlimited, as some do

even today, when evidence to the contrary is plain. To see beyond the assumptions

of our times is a mark of exceptional insight, and Audubon

had this insight, for he not only enjoyed his zestful existence to the full,

he also showed a keen understanding of the need to exercise foresight

in the use of the wildlife resources he studied and loved.

His ornithological biography, the five-volume, octavo-sized

The Birds of America, first published between 1840 and 1844, is full

of warnings about the dire effects of overexploitation.

221
Mallard
Anas platyrhynchos

Although the pintail duck is even
more widely distributed and numerous in the Northern
Hemisphere, the mallard is probably the
world's best-known duck, because it is the only member of
the abundant tribe of Tip-up or Dabbling Ducks
to have been domesticated. These Dabbling Ducks furnish
three-quarters of the bag of waterfowl hunters
worldwide, and the Mallard continues to be the most widely-hunted
duck in North America. "In the Floridas," Audubon
wrote, "they are at times seen in such multitudes as to darken the
air, and the noise they make in rising from
off a large submersed savannah, is like the rumbling of thunder."
One may suppose that there will be Mallards as long
as there are any ducks, but even so abundant
and prolific a species as this one deserves more conservative
management. If the several million hunters of
this bird were to limit their take in years when production
is low, they might more readily grasp the fact that
what will ultimately decide the Mallard's fate is man's
increasing use of the land.

206
Wood Duck
Aix sponsa

Like the almost incredibly sculptured
and colored Mandarin Duck of China, our dainty Wood Duck is
a member of the subfamily of Perching Ducks.
The Muscovy Duck is one of these also, and the group includes several
goose-like species. They all perch in trees
to some extent and have sharp-clawed toes as an aid to clambering among
the branches. The Wood Duck nests in hollow
branches and large woodpecker holes (or nest boxes provided by
man), and the sharp claws enable
its young to climb out of these nesting cavities without difficulty. How do
young Wood Ducks, hatched in a hollow
tree twenty to fifty feet above ground, join their mothers in
order to repair to a nearby pond?
The danger of accepting hearsay evidence is obvious even in the writings
of so careful an observer as Audubon.
He wrote of this event: "If the hole is placed immediately over
the water, the young, the moment they are
hatched, scramble to the mouth of the hole, launch into the air with their
little wings and feet spread out, and
drop into their favorite element; but whenever their birth-place is at
some distance from it, the mother carries
them to it one by one in her bill." No one has actually observed
this transfer, but we know that the ducklings
can and do jump down alone.

246
Common Eider
Somateria mollissima

This is the most impressive of
the Diving Ducks—heavy, squat, well adapted to
riding out gales in the coastal seas that
are its winter home. Eiders are northern nesters, and
Audubon, who arrived on the Labrador
coast too late to witness their courtship, was nevertheless
fascinated by them. He wrote: "Not a single
male did we there see near the females after incubation
had commenced. The males invariably kept aloof and
in large flocks, sometimes of a hundred
or more individuals, remaining out at sea over large banks
with from seven to ten fathoms of water, and
retiring at night to insular rocks." This is the bird
which furnishes the eiderdown of commerce.
In Iceland, the colonies of thousands of eider nests are
carefully husbanded for their down and eggs.
Audubon saw their potential, writing, "I have no
doubt that if this valuable bird were
domesticated, it would prove a great acquisition,
both on account of its feathers and down, and its flesh as an
article of food." Even so, he sounded a warning,
again well ahead of his day: "The eggers of Labrador
usually collect it in considerable quantity,
but at the same time make such havoc
among the birds, that at no very distant period the
traffic must cease."

343
Ruddy Duck
Oxyura jamaicensis

The Ruddy Duck is typical of
the small tribe of Stiff-tailed Ducks which
occur on every continent, of which the
males have chestnut-red plumage in summer, and a
bright blue bill. Audubon was correct
in calling attention to the extreme diversity
of plumages according to age and sex.
He wrote: "Look at this plate, reader, and tell me
whether you ever saw a greater difference
between young and old, or between male and female, than
is apparent here." This helps explain why the bird
has so many vernacular names, and why an old New England
hunter I talked to years ago thought the name
Ruddy Duck ridiculous, since he had never
seen the bird in breeding plumage. Once strictly a
prairie-nester, the Ruddy Duck now nests
in the Northeast, including the Jamaica Bay
Bird Sanctuary in New York City. Because Audubon did
not visit the prairie except in late summer,
he did not know the remarkable courtship displays
of this little stiff-tail, but he did
characterize its normal swimming actions well:
"When swimming without suspicion of danger, they carry
the tail elevated almost perpendicularly,
and float lightly on the water; but as soon as they
are alarmed, they immediately sink deeper . . .
sometimes going out of sight without leaving
a ripple on the water."

51
Red-tailed Hawk
Buteo jamaicensis

As the title of the plate shows,
Audubon called this fine hawk a buzzard, which it is—if we
have any respect for prior use in the matter of names.
For some reason, Americans came to misapply the name "buzzard" to
vultures, thus confusing the nomenclature of birds. Less to the bird's
credit, Audubon's account stresses its characteristics
as a "chicken hawk," in which he followed the folk beliefs of an
agricultural age. At a time when almost every household
kept chickens and let them range freely, perhaps the lure of easy prey
tempted hawks into the habit of pestering farmers' poultry.
Today, definitive studies show clearly that the Red-tailed Hawk
feeds principally on rabbits and mice.
The most Audubon would allow it in this respect was a single short
statement: "I have observed that this species will
even condescend to pounce on woodrats and meadow mice." Part of
this old prejudice, we know now, was due to the failure of
country folk to discriminate among hawks—specifically to recognize
the Cooper's Hawk, which is a true predator of birds.

PLATE LI

91
Broad-winged Hawk
Buteo platypterus

Given the circumstances under which
The Birds of America was written—mostly during intervals in the
preparation of the great elephant folio of engravings,
or on travels—one cannot expect Audubon to have summed up everything he
then knew about birds. But, still, it is surprising that he made
no reference to the spectacular autumnal flights of the
Broad-winged Hawk. Every year, in late August and throughout September,
across the eastern half of North America, birdwatchers keep
an eye to the skies in the hope of enjoying one of these big migratory
movements. Hundreds of birds, sometimes thousands, wheel upward on
thermal air currents, then cruise southward until they encounter another
updraft that will ease their way from north to south,
almost effortlessly, day after day. Because it is a woodland-nester,
seldom perching in the open along roadsides, this smallish
hawk has suffered less from the gun than have its relatives, the Red-tailed
Hawk and the Red-shouldered Hawk, or those northern
and western Buteos, the Rough-legged
Hawks and Swainson's Hawk.

31
Bald Eagle
Haliaeetus leucocephalus

You may remember that
Benjamin Franklin strenuously opposed selecting
this great bird as the emblem of
the United States of America. It is somewhat
surprising that Audubon
agreed with him in this, both men feeling that
an eagle that allowed itself to be
chased by a Kingbird, that robbed the industrious
Osprey of its food, and bore lice,
was not fit to represent this nation. In any
event, being a national symbol has been of no
great help to this bird's survival. Despite
protective laws, we have continued to shoot it, have
even—as in Alaska—paid bounties for
its paired feet, because we begrudged it a
traditional share of the salmon
resource we ourselves were overexploiting.
Worst of all, we have poisoned
its food supplies with DDT; so many eagles now lay eggs
with shells too thin to allow incubation
and hatching, that the species has been seriously
decimated. One wonders whether Mr. Franklin's
objections to the Bald Eagle as
national symbol were not perhaps an allegorical
expression of his concern
about the behavior of his fellow Americans.

81

Osprey
Pandion haliaetus

"The motions of the Fish Hawk in the air are graceful,"
Audubon wrote, "and as majestic as those of the eagle. It rises with
ease to a great height by extensive circlings,
performed apparently by mere inclinations of the wings and tail. It
dives at times to some distance with the wings partially closed, and resumes
its sailing, as if these plunges were made for
amusement only. Whilst in search of food, it flies with easy flappings
at a moderate height above the water, and with an
apparent listlessness, although in reality it is keenly observing the objects
beneath. No sooner does it spy a fish
suited to its taste, than it checks its course with a sudden shake of its
wings and tail, which gives it the appearance of
being poised in the air for a moment, after which it plunges headlong
with rapidity into the water, to secure its prey, or
continues its flight, if disappointed by having observed the fish sink
deeper." Later in the same account, Audubon noted that the
Osprey ". . . has a great attachment to the tree to which it carries its
prey, and will not abandon it, unless
frequently disturbed, or shot at whilst feeding there." This
is an important conservation message.

PLATE

16

Peregrine Falcon
Falco peregrinus

Audubon called this noble bird the
Great-footed Hawk, and for many years
American ornithologists, convinced that our bird
was different from that of Europe, called
it the Duck Hawk. But today we acknowledge that
a single species occurs over most of the
continents, varying regionally, even
locally, so markedly that it is easy to argue for
splitting its populations taxonomically, if
one were so inclined. This is the bird made famous
by falconry over the millennia of man's
civilization—a strong, dashing bird,

whose flight and every demeanor is exciting, even inspiring.
It is a bird-eater, and thus, like the fish-eating Bald Eagle, it stands
at the end of a longer food chain than those of most other species.
The peregrine has been seriously affected by DDT poisoning.
In fact, it was by studying this bird, whose sharp
decline aroused so much concern, that science clarified the mechanisms
of DDT's effects in food chains, and led in 1972 to a ban
on the uses of this pesticide in the United States.
Now attempts are underway to try to re-establish a
breeding population of peregrines in the
eastern United States by the use of birds
produced in captivity.

142

American Kestrel
Falco sparverius

Among American birds of prey, only the Great Horned Owl
equals this little falcon in distribution. Both
of them occur from Alaska to Patagonia, at least seasonally. After
having long called it American Sparrow Hawk,
that name was recently given up in American usage, because
the British had established prior use of
"Sparrowhawk" for a bird closely related to our Sharp-shinned
Hawk. Thus, slowly, do we unravel the babel of
names that makes it so difficult for us to understand one
another. "Every one knows the Sparrow-Hawk,"
Audubon wrote. "The very mention of its name never fails to bring to
mind some anecdote connected with its habits,
and, as it commits no depredations on poultry, few disturb
it, so that the natural increase of the species experiences no check from man."
Again: "Beautifully erect, it stands on the highest fence-stake,
the broken top of a tree, the summit of a grain stack, or the corner of
the barn, patiently and silently waiting until
it spy a mole, a field-mouse, a cricket, or a grasshopper, on
which to pounce." The kestrel nests
in old woodpecker holes and frequently hovers
over its terrestrial prey.

PLATE XLII

American Sparrow Hawk. FALCO SPARVERIUS, Linn. Male 1. Female 2. Butter-nut or White-walnut, Juglans cinerea.

41
Ruffed Grouse
Bonasa umbellus

"If my work deserves the attention
of the public, it must stand on its own legs,
not on the reputation of men
superior in education and literary acquirements,
but possibly not so in the actual observation of nature
at her best, in the wilds, as I certainly have seen her."
This short comment is Audubon's assessment
of himself and it illustrates his desire
to impart reliable information, facts taken from field
observation, and not from reading other
people's books. It is this devotion to facts that made his work,
a century later, "a half-forgotten treasure." Consider
Audubon's account of this grouse.
Of a bird discovered in its haunts he wrote ". . . if
no convenient hiding place is at hand,
it immediately takes flight with as much of the
whirring sound as it can produce,
as if to prove to the observer, that, when on
wing, it cares as little about him
as the deer pretends to do, when on being started by
the hound, he makes several lofty bounds,
and erects his tail to the breeze." He knew from
observation, and contrary to
prevailing opinion, that this whirring flight was
not the only mode of flight, since the
bird can fly softly when it wishes.

Rupped Grous. TETRAO UMBELLUS *Linn. Male & Female.*

186
Greater Prairie Chicken
Tympanuchus cupido

The drastic changes we have made
in the North American continent are well illustrated
by the change of status of this interesting
bird and its immediate relative, the Lesser Prairie
Chicken. The extinct Heath Hen and the Attwater's
Prairie Chicken of the Texas coast
are geographical races of this bird. Together, they
once occurred in great abundance
wherever grasslands provided suitable habitat. The
cultivation of prairie grasslands, from
Ohio westward, has reduced them to relict populations.
However, since they still do well in these
remnant environments, it is obvious that we could
restore their numbers should we at any time value them
enough to restore the grasslands they require.
But, of course, while there are so many
people in competition for space,
such luxurious use of land remains visionary.
Audubon saw this bird disappear from much of
Kentucky in a twenty-five-year period.
"When I first removed to Kentucky," he wrote,
"the Pinnated Grouse were
so abundant, that they were held in no higher
estimation as food than the most
common flesh, and no 'hunter of Kentucky'
deigned to shoot them."

371
Sage Grouse
Centrocercus urophasianus

This largest of our American grouse,
exceeded in size only by the Capercaillie of Eurasia, was
first reported by the Lewis and Clark
Expedition about the time Audubon, in Edinburgh, began
the process of engraving his great work. How he
would have marveled at the stark simplicity of the
Sagebrush Desert of the American Northwest
that is the home of this impressive bird, where "tufted
fields of gray-green sage sweep up to
the sides and walls of the adjacent 'bad lands,' or buttes,
themselves devoid of vegetation but beautiful

in color and fantastic in form."
But Audubon bought specimens of the new birds
collected by Thomas Nuttall and John K.
Townsend on the Lewis and Clark Expedition, and
was thus able to picture them in his
Birds of America. His account gives
these men full credit.
To anyone who has ever examined expeditionary
specimens—stiff and dry, and
with no suggestion of the character of the living
bird—Audubon's artistry in vitalizing
the birds of this painting is impressive indeed.

76
Bobwhite
Colinus virginianus

Whereas the Turkey and the
Prairie Chicken have been much diminished in
numbers by our remaking of the landscape,
Bobwhite populations actually increased for a century
or more, as the birds literally
followed the plow westward, profiting from the
mixed habitats provided by the
small farms which characterized our early agriculture.
They have decreased somewhat in the
last generation, but it is likely that new
changes forced on agriculture by higher energy costs
will soon again benefit this favorite bird.
Also called quail and partridge, the Bobwhite
is a typical member of a distinctive
American subfamily, allied to Old World quail,
partridge, and francolin, and
subsumed with the pheasants in the Family Phasianidae.
It is, therefore, more closely related
to the introduced pheasant than to the native
grouse, which still is sometimes
called partridge in the North. As a game bird,
Bobwhite is to the southern
United States what the Ruffed Grouse is
to the northern tier of States—
a widely distributed, and much-admired bird.

63

1

Turkey
Meleagris gallopavo

The Turkey Cock was the first engraving of Audubon's great
work to be undertaken by William Home Lizars of
Edinburgh. There came later a plate showing the Hen Turkey and
her brood, but the cock bird was selected,
as Audubon wrote in his journal, "to prove the necessity
of the size of the work." (The size referred to was
the "double elephant" folio sheet of paper, nearly four times larger
than quarto book size, which is generous
for most purposes.) The artist wrote this in 1826, and the engraving
of some 512 plates took thirteen years! One of the
dominant scientists of his day, the French Baron Cuvier,
categorized Audubon's great work as "the most magnificent
monument ever erected to nature by art." But this is no more than
the homage paid one famous man by another. What amazes us today
is the incredible drive, versatility, and courage which
Audubon brought to bear—over sixteen long years, often absent from
his family, and beset with the difficulties
of the publication process—in order to produce not only
his extraordinary paintings and engravings,
but the five-volume *Ornithological Biography* and the *Synopsis
of the Birds of North America.*

226

Whooping Crane
Grus americana

Audubon saw this great crane, but he
confused its young with the next species, the Sandhill Crane.
His writings thus gave an incorrect view of
the status of the bird in his day. Since the early
twentieth century, of course, the Whooping Crane has been
a symbol of the wildlife conservation movement. Its wild population
decreased to an apparent low of fourteen birds in 1937, but
an active educational effort to reduce ignorant and wanton shooting
and to protect the bird's breeding and wintering grounds has
forestalled extinction. The wild population—forty-eight birds in early
1974—breeds in Alberta's Wood Buffalo National Park
and winters in an area only partly covered by the Aransas National Wildlife
Refuge in Texas. Seventeen birds have been raised in a captive
breeding program at the Patuxent Wildlife Research Center in
Maryland. The captive population was created mostly by taking one egg from
the double clutch the wild birds lay annually in Canada.
Since these big cranes lay two eggs but usually raise only one
offspring, the effort to make constructive
use of the extra egg seems well directed and promising.

261

Sandhill Crane
Grus canadensis

Great naturalist that he was, Audubon nevertheless
made a serious mistake in not agreeing with other naturalists that
this bird was a distinct species. He insisted that it was
merely the young of the Whooping Crane, and therefore he
grossly exaggerated the numbers of the latter. He was neither the
first nor the last to make such a mistake. There have been
numerous instances in which the immature stage of an already known
species has been wrongly judged as different.
Perhaps Audubon was being overzealous in trying to avoid such
a spurious multiplication of species. We now know that the Sandhill
Crane itself is split into two rather distinct population
units. One is a summer resident of the northern prairie lands of
the United States and Canada; the other nests on the arctic
tundra of northern Canada. The arctic population
is much the larger segment, amounting to over 200,000 birds in
most years. Numbers fluctuate considerably, because
the tundra is a harsh breeding ground. At present the Platte River
bottoms, in Nebraska, are a key migration stop.

69

205
Virginia Rail
Rallus limicola

Writing of spring migrants, Audubon said,
"As soon as they arrive . . . they may be heard emitting their cries
about sunset, occasionally through the night,
and again with increased vigor at the dawn of day, as if
expressing their impatience for the arrival
of their companions. Being expert ventriloquists, like their
congeners (the Clapper and King Rails),
they sometimes seem to be far off, when in fact they are within a few
yards of you. One morning . . . the notes of the rail came
loudly on my ear, and on moving toward the spot . . . I observed
the bird exhibiting the full ardor of his passion.
Now with open wings raised over its body, it ran around its beloved,
opening and flirting its tail with singular speed. Each time
it passed before her, it would pause for a moment, raise itself to
the full stretch of its body and legs, and bow to her with all the grace
of a well-bred suitor of our own species. The female
also bowed in recognition, and at last, as the male came nearer and
nearer in his circuits, yielded to his wishes, on which
the pair flew off in the manner of house pigeons, sailing
and balancing their bodies on open wings."

PLATE. CCV.

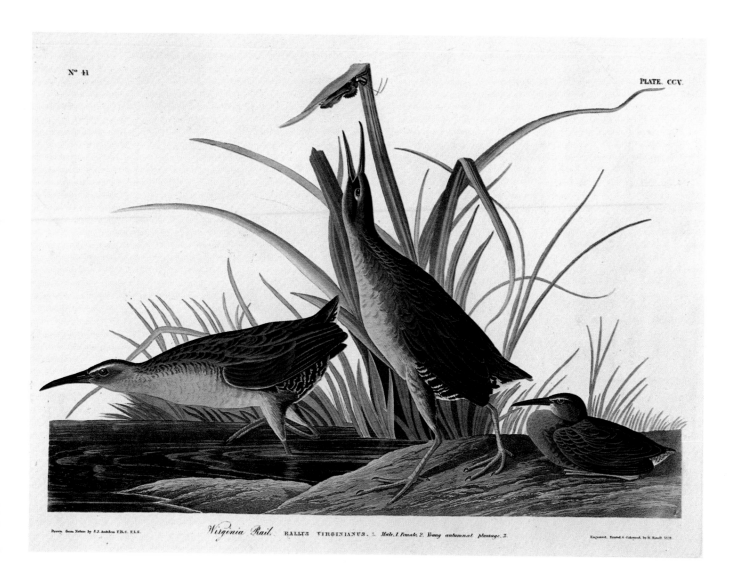

Drawn from Nature by J.J.Audubon F.R.S. F.L.S. *Virginia Rail.* RALLUS VIRGINIANUS. 1. *Male,1.Female, 2. Young autumnal plumage, 3.* Engraved, Printed & Coloured, by R. Havell 1835.

209
Wilson's Plover
Charadrius wilsonia

"Reader," Audubon wrote, "imagine
yourself standing motionless on some of the
sandy shores between South Carolina
and the extremity of Florida, waiting with impatience
for the return of the day—or if you dislike
the idea, imagine me there. The air is warm and
pleasant, the smooth sea reflects the feeble
glimmerings of the fading stars, the sound of a
living thing is not heard; nature,
universal nature, is at rest. And here I am inhaling
the grateful sea-air, with eyes intent on
the dim distance. . . . Well, let the
scene vanish! and let me present you with the

results of my observations.
Wilson's Plover! I love the name because of the
respect I bear towards him to whose
memory the bird has been dedicated. How pleasing,
I have thought, it would have been
to me, to have met with him on such an excursion,
and, after having procured a few of his
own birds, to have listened to him as he would
speak of a thousand interesting facts
connected with his favorite science and my
everlasting pursuits." Thus does
Audubon lead us onward in his ornithological
biography, *The Birds of America*.

225
Killdeer
Charadrius vociferus

This handsome plover of open
pastures and watercourses occurs across southern
Canada and the entire contiguous
United States in summer, and retires for the
winter to Central America. "The Killdeer," Audubon
wrote, "is by most people called a 'noisy bird
and restless.' Now to me it is
anything but this, unless indeed when it
is disturbed by the approach or appearance of its
enemies, more particularly man, of whom
indeed few wild birds are fond. Watch them from
under some cover that completely
conceals you, and you will see them peaceably
and silently follow their avocations for hours.
In this respect the Killdeer resembles
the Lapwing of Europe, which is also called
a restless and noisy bird, because men
and dogs are ever in pursuit of the poor thing.
During winter, when undisturbed, the
Killdeer is in fact an unusually silent bird."
It is curious that, although he knew
it well, Audubon did not seem to distinguish
what we now call the "distraction
display" of this common bird.

Nº 45.

Drawn from Nature by J.J.Audubon, F.R.S. F.L.S.

PLATE. CCXXV.

Engraved. Printed.& Coloured.by R.Havell. 1834.

Kildeer Plover. CHARADRIUS VOCIFERUS. *1.Male. 2.Female.*

268

American Woodcock
Philohela minor

This bird, which sportsmen call a "Timberdoodle,"
is really a highly specialized upland
sandpiper. Its long bill is flexible for the last inch or
so of its length; after probing it deeply
into soft ground, the bird can "gape," or expand, it
to snatch its prey, whether a grub or an
earthworm. Specialization is further shown by the
large, dark eye placed high on the head,
and the fact that the ear is below the eye, not behind
it. What makes this dumpy bird so
delightful for many of us is its springtime flight song.
In the region surrounding New York City,
this may be heard at dusk during the last two weeks
of March, if suitable brushy fields are visited.
The male repeats a "peent" note while on the ground and
at intervals ascends steeply into the graying sky,
his wings whistling shrilly. After a few moments of circling,
he pitches back to the same grassy territory with a
"chippering" chatter. This courtship display Audubon
referred to as "curious spiral gyrations."

243

Common Snipe
Capella gallinago

Naturalists of Audubon's time had a great
enthusiasm for separating recognizable forms into
different species (and incidentally claiming authorship for
the distinction). Alexander Wilson—who vied with
Audubon for a while as the foremost student of American
birds—described this bird as different, and until
recently it was called Wilson's Snipe. Today, however, the
trend is in the other direction; geographical
varieties are being "lumped" as subspecies of a single
species. We now recognize this snipe as a mere
variant of a species spread circumboreally. "When surprised
by the sportsman, or any other enemy,"
Audubon wrote, "they usually rise at one spring,
dash through the air in a zig-zag course, a few feet from
the ground, emit their cry when about twenty
yards distant, and at times continue to employ this cunning
mode of escape for sixty or seventy yards, after
which they mount into the air . . . fly around a few times . . .
pitch towards the ground, and alight,
with the velocity of an arrow, not many yards from
the spot where they had previously been."

Nº 49.

Drawn from Nature, by J.J. Audubon.

PLATE. CCXLIII.

American Snipe Male 1 Female 2,3
SCOLOPAX WILSONII,
South Carolina Plantation near Charleston.

Engraved, Printed, & Coloured, by R. Havell, London, 1835.

231
Long-billed Curlew
Numenius americanus

Audubon got to know this most impressive
of our shore birds only on its wintering grounds or in
migration, never during its nesting time, when
it animated most of the interior prairies of North America.
When the prairies were taken over for
agriculture, beginning in the early 1850's, this bird's breeding
range was cut in half, and so also were its
numbers. Today the Long-billed Curlew is rare east of the
Mississippi. But in November, 1831, Audubon
could make note of a typical roosting flight of these big
curlews outside Charleston, South Carolina: "When
we followed them to the Bird Banks, which are sandy islands of
small extent, the moment they saw us land, the
congregated flocks, probably amounting to several thousand
individuals all standing close together, rose at
once, performed a few evolutions in perfect silence, and
re-alighted as if with one accord on the
extreme margins of the sandbank close to tremendous breakers.
It was now dark, and we left the place, although some
flocks were still arriving. . . ."

238
Marbled Godwit
Limosa fedoa

It is difficult to reconstruct the
former status of such grassland-nesters as the
Long-billed Curlew and the Marbled Godwit,
so drastically has their favored habitat been altered
in the last century. Audubon knew the
eastern extension of the prairie but not
the northern prairies of central North America.
He therefore never saw these birds on their nesting
grounds. His observation of a large
gathering of "some thousands" of birds in Florida
Bay in May of 1832 was perhaps a fortuitous
occurrence even then. Or, were there indeed so
many of these shore birds then
that they rimmed the Gulf of Mexico as they made their
way to or from wintering grounds in
Central America? Today they are rare in the East,
and the principal migratory movements
are toward the Gulf of California. What handsome
birds they are—stalking the beaches, erect
and alert, ever ready to fly strongly when disturbed!
The slightly upturned bill distinguishes
godwits from curlews, but it is intriguing that
both this species and its neighbor on the
nesting grounds, the Long-billed
Curlew, have cinnamon-colored wing linings.

PLATE CCXXXVIII.

Great Marbled Godwit. 1 Male. 2 Female.
LIMOSA FEDOA. Vieill.

Engraved, Printed & Coloured by R. Havell. London. 1835.

318
American Avocet
Recurvirostra americana

Today one expects to see avocets only
under the big skies and intense light of western
North America, but in Audubon's day
they nested all the way to the Atlantic Coast,
except in the Northeast. There is
little question that the gun pushed them out of
their early haunts, but today protection has made
what remains of our eastern open spaces
attractive enough to induce these colorful, almost
stilt-legged shore birds to return regularly
to the wet meadows of southern New Jersey and elsewhere
farther south. We may confidently expect
them to nest here in the coming years, just as Audubon
found them nesting near Vincennes, Indiana,
in 1814. Of these birds he wrote: "They kept apart,
but crossed each other's path in hundreds of ways,
all perfectly silent, and without showing
the least symptom of enmity towards each other. They
search for food precisely in the manner
of the Roseate Spoonbill, moving their heads to
and fro sideways, while their bill
is passing through the soft mud; and in many
instances, when the water was deeper,
they would immerse their whole head and a
portion of the neck."

17
Mourning Dove
Zenaidura macroura

Despite much bluster to the contrary,
the fortunes of this bird suggest that the meek
shall indeed inherit the earth.
It is tragic that the Passenger Pigeon, whose
amazing legions Audubon described
from notes made in Kentucky about 1815, is now extinct.
But it could apparently not be otherwise,
since the colonists—medieval agriculturists that they
were—had to cut the forests that housed and
nourished these legions. The birds traditionally
associated in such huge companies that they succumbed
to the partitioning of their range.
The Mourning Dove, on the other hand, was always more
widespread, always dispersed in modest numbers,
and thus less vulnerable to persecution. Indeed,
as we destroyed the forests' carrying
capacity for the Passenger Pigeon, we made them more
suitable for the Mourning Dove. It is
now the most widely dispersed game bird in America,
is prolific, and thus supplies more "birds
in the bag" than any other species.
Some observers, overlooking the implications of population
biology, continue to fear that hunting
pressure may yet exterminate the dove—as it
did the pigeon—but there is little
evidence to support such a view.

171

Barn Owl
Tyto alba

The half-opened wing, seen to such advantage in this
painting and in those of the Screech Owl and the Broad-winged
Hawk, is a delightful convention invented by the artist
to combine what we already know of birds
with what he has to show us. That Audubon had these objectives in
mind is easily seen from his prospectus of the great work.
Of his paintings he said: "It may be proper to state that their
superiority consists in the accuracy as to proportion
and outline, and the variety and truth of the
attitudes and positions of the figures, resulting from the peculiar
means discovered and employed by the author, by his
attentive examination of the objects portrayed during a long
series of years. The author has not contented himself, as others have
done, with single profile views, but in very many
instances has grouped his figures so as to represent the originals
at their natural avocations, and has placed them on branches of trees,
decorated with foliage, blossoms, and fruits, or amidst plants
of numerous species. Some are pursuing
their prey through the air . . . ."

97

Screech Owl

Otus asio

Why this gentle bird, whose song
is an easily imitated, tremulous wail or whistle, should have been
misnamed Screech Owl is difficult to understand.
The confusion has been compounded even more because it comes in gray,
brown, and reddish color phases, sometimes all in one nest. Even
Audubon, though he criticized his rival Alexander Wilson
for confusing the issue, did not appreciate that these were true
color phases, not matters of age, as he thought.
So we are told, in one of Audubon's few errors, "You are presented,
dear reader, with three figures of this species, the better to show
you the differences which exist between the young and
the full-grown bird. The contrast of coloring in these different
stages I have thought it necessary to exhibit,
as the Red Owl of Wilson and other naturalists is merely the young of
the bird called by the same authors the Mottled Owl,
and which, in fact, is the adult of the species under consideration.
The error committed by the author of the *American Ornithology* [Wilson],
for many years misled all subsequent students of nature."

PLATE XCVI

Little Screech Owl. STRIX ASIO *Linn. Adult 1. Young 2.3. Jersey Pine Pinus inops.*

61
Great Horned Owl
Bubo virginianus

If early, self-sustaining farmers had any bird
to fear, it was this representative of the nearly cosmopolitan
genus *Bubo*. As Audubon saw well, "Differences of
locality are no security against the depredations of this owl, for it
occurs in the highest mountain districts, as well as in the
low alluvial lands that border the rivers, in the
interior of the country and in the neighborhood of the sea-shore."
Even so, except for those unwilling to exercise a modicum
of care in housing their small animals, this bird's depredations
are traditionally overstated. Although it has the strength
and courage to tackle birds as large
as half-grown turkeys, the bulk of its food is composed of items
the size of mice and rabbits. Like most predators, this
big owl is an opportunist and must depend for its everyday
diet on what is most abundant and easy to take. Mice and rabbits
satisfy these criteria, so they are dietary staples.
Except for larger animals—which they dismember—all owls
tend to swallow their prey whole, fur and bones included. Later they
regurgitate the rough indigestible fragments in pellet form.

46

Barred Owl
Strix varia

"Such persons as conclude, when
looking upon owls in the glare of the day, that
they are, as they then appear, extremely dull, are greatly
mistaken." One of the great ornithologists of this country, Robert
Cushman Murphy, once called the ornithological
biography of Audubon a "half-forgotten treasure," and these glimpses
of the artist's feeling for and knowledge of the birds
he studied three half-centuries ago, which are abstracted here, are
witness to the soundness of this judgment. "How often," Audubon
wrote, "when snugly settled under the boughs of my temporary encampment,
and preparing to roast a venison steak or the body of
a squirrel, have I been saluted with the exulting bursts of this nightly
disturber of the peace. How often have I seen this nocturnal marauder
alight within a few yards of me, expose his whole body to
the glare of my fire, and eye me in such a curious
manner that, had it been reasonable to do so, I would gladly have
invited him to walk in and join me in my repast . . .
his society would be at least as agreeable as that of many
of the buffoons we meet in the world."

425

Anna's Hummingbird
Calypte anna

When Audubon wrote his accounts of the
country's hummingbirds, only four of our fourteen species had
been discovered, and he knew only the
Ruby-throated Hummingbird from field experience. There are
more than three hundred species of this amazing,
strictly American family, most of them residents of South and Central America.
We have learned a great deal about them since
Audubon's day, but none of this family's unique characteristics is
more amazing than the ability of several species,
including Anna's Hummingbird, to hibernate overnight. This trait involves
lowering the body temperature and assuming a state of
complete torpidity, so that the bird
appears to have died on its perch. This is done not because of cold
weather, but to avoid the consequences of
cold weather, which otherwise would require the bird to exhaust
its energy supplies in order to maintain its normally
high temperature. It is an energy-conserving tactic. Torpidity
in birds—it now seems—was reported a
hundred years before science
was willing to accept it.

PLATE CCCCXXV.

Drawn from Nature by J.J. Audubon, F.R.S. F.L.S.

Columbian Humming Bird.
TROCHILUS ANNA, *Lesson*
1, 2, 3 & 4 Male. 5 Female and Nest.
Plant, Hibiscus Virginicus

Engraved, Printed and Coloured by Rob.ᵗ Havell 1838.

PLATE

37
Common Flicker
Colaptes auratus

Until the check-list committee of
the American Ornithologists' Union—the arbiter in such
matters—released its 1973 deliberation on the relationships and
names of American birds, three species of flickers were
listed in North America: the Yellow-shafted Flicker in the East,
the Red-shafted Flicker in the West, and the Gilded
Flicker in the deserts of the Southwest. However, since they all
interbreed to some extent wherever their ranges come
together, we now accept the fact that they constitute a single
species; hence the common name. This, of course,
has not changed the birds themselves, and we may continue to
label our particular subspecies—the regional
populations—by their old common names. Audubon's observations
were affectionate: "Even in confinement," he wrote,
"the Golden-winged Woodpecker never suffers its naturally lively
spirit to droop. It feeds well, and by way of amusement,
will continue to destroy as much furniture in a
day as can well be mended by a different
kind of workman in two."

PLATE XX

Golden-winged Woodpecker.

PICUS AURATUS, Linn.

Males, 1. Females, 2.

d Published by John J. Audubon, F.R.S.F.L.S.

Engraved, Printed, & Coloured by R. Havell.

111

Pileated Woodpecker
Dryocopus pileatus

Early in the present century it was
feared that this great woodpecker would follow the
Ivory-billed Woodpecker into oblivion. But
with the regrowth of forest on millions of acres of abandoned
farmland in the Northeast it has increased again
to safe numbers. Audubon's account demonstrates the detailed
investigation he lavished on all the birds he was
able to study. "The observation of many years has convinced me,"
he wrote, "that woodpeckers of all sorts have the bill
longer when just fledged than at any future period of their life,
and that through use it becomes not only shorter,
but also much harder, stronger, and sharper. When the woodpecker
first leaves the nest, its bill may easily be
bent; six months after, it resists the force of the fingers;
and when the bird is twelve months old,
the organ has acquired its permanent bony hardness. On
measuring the bill of a young bird of this
species not long able to fly, and that of an adult bird,
I found the former seven-eights of an inch
longer than the latter."

PLATE CX

Pileated Woodpecker
PICUS PILEATUS, *Linn.*
Adult Male 1, Adult Female 2, Young Males 3, 4.

27
Red-headed Woodpecker
Melanerpes erythrocephalus

These birds were so common that
Audubon apologized to his readers, "Were I assured of
your having traversed the woods of America, I
should feel disposed to say little about them." This is unfortunately
no longer true in much of the Northeast, evidently because
the automobile has killed too many of these low-flying birds, and because
the introduced Starling has appropriated too many of their
nesting places. A pity, too, because it is a cheery bird. As Audubon
put it: "With the exception of the Mockingbird, I know no
species so gay and frolicksome. Indeed, their
whole life is one of pleasure. They find a superabundance of food
everywhere, as well as the best facilities for raising
their broods. They do not seem to be much afraid of man although they
have scarcely a more dangerous enemy. When alighted on a
fence-stake by the road, or in a field, and one approaches them,
they gradually move sidewise out of sight, peeping now
and then to discover your intention; and when you are quite
close and opposite, lie still until you are past, when
they hop to the top of the stake, and rattle upon
it, as if to congratulate themselves on their cunning."

Drawn from Nature & Published by John J. Audubon. F.R.S.E.L.S.

Engraved, Printed & Coloured by R. H.

Red headed Woodpecker.

PICUS ERYTHROCEPHALUS, Linn.

Male 1. Female 2. Young 3.

173
Barn Swallow
Hirundo rustica

"They play over the river,
the field, or the city with equal grace, and during
spring and summer you might imagine
their object was to fill the air around them with their
cheerful twitterings. . . . The nest is attached
to the side of a beam or rafter in a barn or shed, under
a bridge, or sometimes even in an old well,
or in a sink hole, such as those found in the Kentucky
barrens. Whenever the situation is convenient
and affords sufficient room, you find
several nests together, and in some instances I have seen
seven or eight within a few inches of each
other; nay, in some large barns I have counted forty,
fifty, or more. The male and the female both
betake themselves to the borders of creeks, rivers, ponds, or
lakes, where they form small pellets of mud
or moist earth, which they carry in their bill to the chosen
spot, and place against the wood, the wall, or
the rock, as it may chance to be. They dispose of these
pellets in regular layers, mixing, especially
with the lower, a considerable
quantity of long, slender grasses."

PLATE. CLXXIII

Barn Swallow.
HIRUNDO RUSTICA.
Male. 1. Female. 2.

Drawn from Nature by J.J. Audubon FRS. FLS.

Engraved, Printed & Coloured, by R. Havell 1833.

102
Blue Jay
Cyanocitta cristata

Paradoxically, many people refuse to
make inferences about human behavior from behaviorisms
widespread in the animal kingdom, yet they
judge the other animals as if they were humans. Even Audubon
gives in to this tendency: "Who could imagine that
a form so graceful, arrayed by nature in a garb so resplendent,
should harbor so much mischief—that selfishness,
duplicity, and malice should form the moral accompaniments of so much
physical perfection! Yet so it is, and how like beings
of a much higher order, are these gay deceivers!" The role of jays in the
community of birds surely varies from place to place and from
time to time, but it is useful to keep a gamut of evidence in mind. For example,
in Bent's *Life Histories of North American Jays, Crows, and Titmice*
an early observer is quoted thus: "To those who know
the Blue Jay only as a wild, shy bird of the tree-tops, so hard to approach,
or, by reputation, as a thief or a robber of other
bird's nests, there remains a pleasure like unto finding
some new and rare bird, to watch a pair of jays
through the nesting season and to find them so devoted to their
nest and young that they lose much of their shyness."

Blue Jay,

CORVUS CRISTATUS,

Male. 1. Female. 2.3.

nature by J.J. Audubon F.R.S. F.L.S.

Engraved, printed & Coloured

87
Scrub Jay
Aphelocoma coerulescens

The Scrub Jays—until recently
known by at least twelve confusing common names—
are now more sensibly treated as a group. Audubon knew and
wrote about a separate population in Florida, then called the Florida
Jay. So drastic has been our remaking of Florida's
landscape in the last generation that there is cause for concern
about the future existence of these regional dwellers.
Audubon's plate illustrates the tendency of birds of close
habitats—woodland or scrub growth—to have blunt wings. This results
from evolutionary pressure, whereby there is a
shortening of the primary flight feather at the forward edge of the wing.
Ironically, anatomists call this not the first but the
tenth primary. A blunt wing permits greater flight maneuverability
in close quarters and is in distinct contrast
to the long, pointed wing one sees in open-country birds, such
as swallows and shore birds. Audubon observed
these things but could not explain them. Only in our generation
has growing knowledge of evolution and aeronautical
principles clarified these functions.

Florida Jay

CORVUS FLORIDANUS, *Bartram.*

Male 1. Female 2.

Persimon Tree, Diospyros virginiana.

Drawn from Nature and Published by John J. Audubon, F.R.S.F.L.S.

Engraved, Printed & Coloured by R. Havell.

357
Black-billed Magpie
Pica pica

Magpies, like jays and several
related groups (about 112 species), are members of the Family
of Crows (Corvidae). Many consider the members
of this Family the most highly evolved or advanced birds, citing
their intelligence, adaptability, and social organization
as evidence. (This would place them last in the
check-list order and therefore last to be described
in this book. However the sparrows have not yet officially been
displaced as the most advanced Family, and so
they retain the final—honored—place in this gallery of species.)
Whereas this magpie occurs across Eurasia,
in North America it is restricted to the Northwest. It seems obvious
that it invaded North America through Alaska following
the last great Ice Age and that it has not yet had time to spread
across our country. A related form, the Yellow-billed
Magpie, has penetrated California's valleys and foothills. Audubon
gave it the name of its discoverer, Thomas Nuttall, so that
its technical name is *Pica nuttalli*, denoting a separate
species. Someday, however, after more comparative
study, it may be reduced to subspecies rank,
whereupon it will be *Pica pica nuttalli*.

PLATE 6

American Magpie?

CORVUS PICA?

Male 1. Female 2

98
Long-billed Marsh Wren
Telmatodytes palustris

"It is a homely, little bird,
and is seldom noticed, unless by the naturalist,
when searching for other species, or by children, who in all
countries are fond of birds." This statement of Audubon's reminds
us that curiosity is innate—though few exercise
it constructively after childhood. Children, especially boys,
are predators by nature, and most of us would
agree that we achieve our measure of intimacy with nature
through this instinct to hunt. Reflection on these things—which leads
first to art and then to science—requires a degree of leisure
and freedom from material needs. Knowing this, could we not easily
design a society that would foster the artist's appreciation
and the scientist's understanding of nature? All preaching is
wasted if circumstances do not favor expression.
Many of Audubon's followers in conservation seem to have
overlooked this. These "homely little birds"
are doubly intriguing in that the male, first to arrive on
the nesting grounds, builds from one to five
"dummy" nests before a female settles in with him and
completes one for her brood.

PLATE C

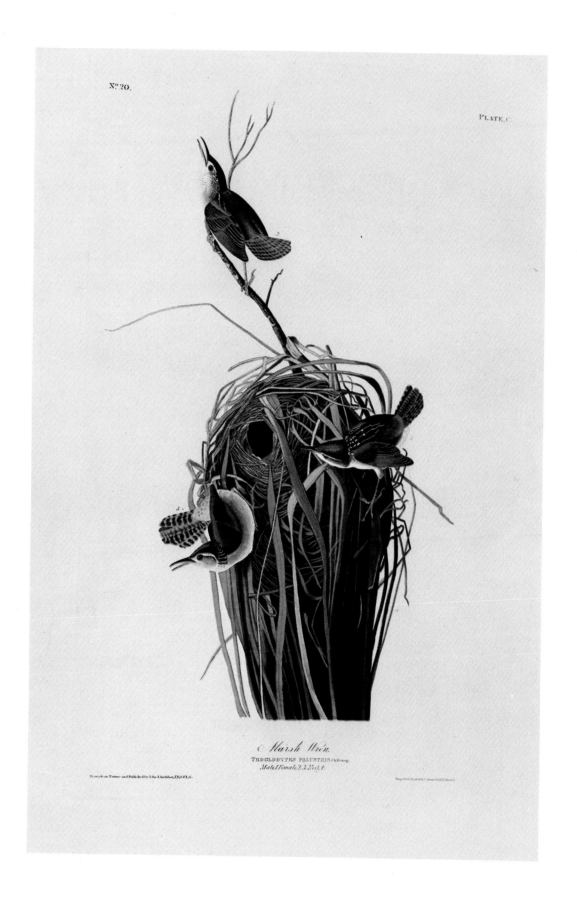

Marsh Wren.
TROGLODYTES PALUSTRIS. *(Ch.Bonap.)*
Male 1.Female, 2.3. Nest 4.

Drawn from Nature and Published by John J.Audubon, F.R.S.F.L.S.

Engraved Printed & Coloured by R.Havell

21
Mockingbird
Mimus polyglottos

No other American bird species
has so many champions. Audubon waxed ecstatic over
its contribution to the landscape and felt that to fully appreciate
it, one had to hear this virtuoso in Louisiana.
His testimony must have made a profound imprint on American
taste, for—remember—Audubon's five-volume
work was the greatest compendium of popular ornithology for nearly
a century. The modern compendium is Arthur Cleveland
Bent's *Life Histories of North American Birds*, published in twenty-two
volumes between 1919 and 1968 as Bulletins of
the United States National Museum. A century after Audubon wrote
about the mockers of Louisiana, a contributor to
Bent's *Life Histories*, Alexander Sprunt, Jr., reminded everyone
that South Carolina had a proprietary interest in
this bird. Had not naturalist Mark Catesby introduced the species
to science more than two hundred years ago with
a specimen from the Carolina Low Country? And were not the
ornithological and botanical glories of the
Pelican State, which Audubon discoursed upon, equally
accurate descriptions of the environs of
Charleston? Of course, Sprunt was a Charlestonian.

128
Gray Catbird
Dumetella carolinensis

How unfortunate that a name, even
a misnomer, should prejudice us against another even before
we come to know it. I was so surprised by Audubon's
testimony on this score that I consulted other sources and found that,
sure enough, many admit to an early prejudice against
the Catbird. Was I more open than most, or has my fondness for this
bird obliterated any adverse feelings I might have
had toward its name? Here is what Audubon wrote: "The vulgar name
which this species bears . . . has also served to bring it into
some degree of contempt with persons not the best judges of the benefits
it confers on the husbandman in early spring, when, with
industrious care, it cleanses his fruit-trees of thousands of larvae and
insects, which, in a single day, would destroy, while
yet in the bud, far more of his fruit than the Catbird would eat in a whole
season. But alas, selfishness, the usual attendant of
ignorance, not only heaps maledictions on this harmless bird, but
dooms it to destruction. The boys pelt the poor
thrush with stones, and destroy its nest whenever an opportunity
presents; the farmer shoots it to save a pear; and the
gardener to save a raspberry; some hate it, not knowing why."

Cat Bird.
TURDUS FELIVOX.
Male 1. Female 2.
Plant Rising - Rubus villosus.

PLATE

116

Brown Thrasher

Toxostoma rufum

Audubon has sometimes been
accused of exaggerating the postures and dramatic effects of
his paintings, but this spirited plate merely takes
advantage of a real-life drama which he had observed and which others
have observed after him, even though it may not be
a common experience. Thrashers, like Catbirds and Mockingbirds,
are called mimic thrushes because they imitate the songs of other birds.
Although this is true, we are perhaps inclined to
overstate the tendency. It seems from careful study that only about ten
percent of the songs of the best mimic in the
group—the mockingbird itself—are true mimicry, and that such
songs usually imitate those of other species the
mimic hears regularly. Indeed, it is often in putting our assumptions
to the test of study that new and unsuspected facts
emerge. In 1974, for example, it was demonstrated that some
small songbirds actually adjust the timing
of their songs to avoid overlapping those of their
neighbors. This makes good sense,
since the object of song, of course, is to be heard.

131

American Robin
Turdus migratorius

"Whenever the sun shines warmly over the earth,"
Audubon wrote, "the old males tune their pipe, and enliven
the neighborhood with their song. The young also begin to sing;
and, before they depart for the east, they have all
become musical. By the tenth of April, the robins have reached
the Middle Districts; the blossoms of the dogwood are then peeping forth
in every part of the budding woods; the fragrant sassafras,
the red flowers of the maple, and hundreds of other plants, have already
banished the dismal appearance of winter. The snows are all
melting away, and nature again, in all the beauty of spring, promises
happiness and abundance to the whole animal creation. Then it
is that the robin, perched on a fence-stake, or the top of some detached
tree of the field, gives vent to the warmth of his passion.
His lays are modest, lively, and oftimes of considerable power; and
although his song cannot be compared with that of the
thrasher, its vivacity and simplicity never fail to fill the
breast of the listener with pleasing sensations.
Everyone knows the robin and his song."

73
Wood Thrush
Catharus mustelina

Audubon described this bird as
"my greatest favorite of the feathered tribes of our woods,"
and continued: "The song of the Wood Thrush, although
composed of but few notes, is so powerful, distinct, clear, and mellow,
that it is impossible for any person to hear it without
being struck by the effect it produces on the mind. I do not know
to what instrumental sounds I can compare these notes. . . . They gradually
rise in strength, and then fall in gentle cadences, becoming at
length so low as to be scarcely audible. Several of these birds seem to
challenge each other from different portions of the
forest, particularly towards evening, and at that time nearly all the other
songsters being about to retire to rest, the notes of the Wood
Thrush are doubly pleasing. One would think that each individual is
anxious to excel his distant rival, and I have frequently
thought that on such occasions their music is more than ordinarily
effective, as it then exhibits a degree of skillful
modulation quite beyond my power to describe.
These concerts are continued for some time after sunset,
and take place in the month of June, when
the females are sitting."

Wood Thrush.
TURDUS MUSTELINUS, *Gmel.*
Male, 1. Female, 2.
Dogwood. Cornus florida.

Drawn from Nature and Published by John J. Audubon, F.R.S.F.L.S.   Engraved, Printed & Coloured by R. Havell.

113
Eastern Bluebird
Sialia sialis

It often comes as a surprise that our Bluebird
is a thrush, though there is a clue in the fact that its young,
like those of the Robin, have a spotted
breast. The Thrush Family's nearly three hundred species
are divisible into two large groups: the robin-like
thrushes, of which our American Robin is typical, and the smaller,
slender-legged chat-like thrushes. Our three American
bluebird species belong to this second group, as does the European Robin.
These classifying details aside, bluebirds are
everywhere favorites. Audubon's description is appropriate: "Full
of innocent vivacity, warbling its ever pleasing notes, and
familiar as any bird can be in its natural
freedom, it is one of the most agreeable of our feathered favorites.
The pure azure of its mantle, and the beautiful glow
of its breast, render it conspicuous, as it flits through the orchards
and gardens, crosses the fields or meadows,
or hops along by the roadside." It is unfortunately less common
than it once was, due to the elimination of small
orchards, competition from the House Sparrow,
and chemical pesticides.

PLATE CXIII

Blue-bird,
SYLVIA SIALIS,
Male 1. Female 2. Young 3.
Great Mullein, Verbascum Thapsus.

Drawn from Nature by J.J.Audubon F.R.S. F.L.S.

Engraved, Printed & Coloured by R. Havell London. 1831.

43
Cedar Waxwing
Bombycilla cedrorum

This sleek, silky-plumaged, widespread small bird
gives us some cause to ask what other bird artists have thought
of Audubon. It is useless to try to measure one against another, but
let Louis Agassiz Fuertes, the greatest painter of birds
of the twentieth century, tell us—in a letter written in 1917—
how he reacted to Audubon's work. Fuertes was
brought up in Ithaca, New York, where—fortuitously—there was a set of
Audubon's elephant-folio plates in the town library.
Of it Fuertes wrote: "This set was for ten years or more my
daily bread; by it I was thrilled so that
it melts me now to remember it, and many—so very many—of the
plates are still as familiar to me as the wallpaper
in the hall of the first house I remember living in! By those lovingly
done things I was moved—and still am—in a
way I would find it hard to express. For most of these bore the
authentic stamp of the fresh bird—and his ardor was
so transparent to me, and mine so responded to it, that I could
never do other than admit the enormous influence
on my own aching ardency to 'go and do likewise.'"

Cedar Bird.
BOMBYCILLA CAROLINENSIS, Brifs.
Male, 1. Female, 2.
Red Cedar Juniperus virginiana.

35
Yellow Warbler
Dendroica petechia

Since intelligence, dangerous word though it is,

means action conjoined to perception, see if you don't agree

that the little Yellow Warbler must be accounted more

intelligent than many other living beings of your choice. Reporting

the observations of his friend, Dr. Thomas M. Brewer

of Boston, Audubon wrote: "There is a very interesting item in

the history of the Yellow-poll Warbler, which

has been noticed only within a few years, and which is well deserving

of attention, both for the reasoning powers which it exhibits,

and for its uniqueness, for it is not known, I believe,

to be practiced by any other bird. I allude to the surprising

ingenuity with which they often contrive to escape the burden of rearing

the offspring of the Cowbird, by burying the egg of the

intruder. I have known four instances in which single eggs have

been thus buried by the Yellowbird's building a second

story to her nest, and enclosing the intruder between them."

In one instance, he reported, three of the

Warbler's own eggs were covered along with the Cowbird's egg;

the final result was a three-storied structure.

PLATE XXXV

Drawn from Nature and Published by John J. Audubon, F.R.S.E.L.S.

Childrens Warbler.

Engraved Printed & Coloured by R. Havell.

SYLVIA CHILDRENII, Aud.

Male, 1. Female, 2.

Wild Spanish Coffee Cassia occidentalis.

136
Eastern Meadowlark
Sturnella magna

This was a favorite bird of Colonial America
and of the small-farm and small-town era that persisted
almost until World War II. Its popularity has
decreased only because there is less opportunity for most
of us to enjoy it. Audubon recalled the pleasant memories of his
own youth as he wrote of this bird: "When the Meadowlark
first rises from the ground, which it does with a smart spring,
it flutters like a young bird, then proceeds checking its
speed and resuming it in a desultory and uncertain manner, flying in
general straight forward, and glancing behind as if to ascertain
the amount of its danger, but yet affording an easy
aim to the most inexperienced marksman. When pursued for awhile,
it moves more swiftly, sailing and beating its
wings alternately, until it gets out of reach." Of the nest, usually
placed at the foot of some tuft of tall, strong
grass, he wrote, "A cavity is scooped out of the ground, and
in it is placed a quantity of grass, fibrous roots,
and other materials, circularly disposed so
as to resemble an oven."

67
Red-winged Blackbird
Agelaius phoeniceus

Corn and rice growers still have difficulties with
this otherwise attractive bird, especially if they carelessly
try to produce in the wrong places—adjacent to large marshes, or on a
migratory flyway. In Audubon's day, when almost everyone
grew corn and when rice culture was as important in the
South as it is today, this blackbird was widely regarded as a pest.
He wrote: "The Marsh Blackbird is so well known
as being a bird of the most nefarious propensities, that in
the United States one can hardly mention its name, without hearing such an
account of its pilferings as might induce the young student
of nature to conceive that it had been created for
the purpose of annoying the farmer. That it destroys an astonishing
quantity of corn, rice, and other kinds of grain, cannot be
denied; that before it commences its ravages, it has
proved highly serviceable to the crops, is equally certain.
The millions of insects which the Redwings destroy at this early
season [spring], are, in my opinion, a full equivalent
for the corn which they eat at another period."

Red winged Starling or Marsh Blackbird.

ICTERUS PHOENICEUS, Daud.

Adult Male.1.Young Male.2.Female Old.3.Young.1.

Red Maple, or Swamp Maple. Acer rubrum.

r. and Publish'd by John J. Audubon. F.R.S.E.L.S.

Engraved, Printed & Coloured by R. Havell

12

Northern Oriole
Icterus galbula

To many people it came as a
surprise that the familiar and much-loved Baltimore
Oriole of the eastern United States,
and the West's favorite counterpart, Bullock's Oriole, are
so closely related that scientists have judged
them to be the same species. Although distinctive in adult male
plumage, and thus easily separated in the field,
they interbreed where their ranges overlap, and it is this failure
to be reproductively isolated, by behavior or structure,
that is taken to indicate that they are merely geographic races of
the same species. So now the bird books will refer to
both of them under this single name, but we may, of course, continue
to call them by the long-familiar personal names, each
to his own. Audubon's painting shows the distinctive hanging nest
of these orioles—a family trait, because their tropical
relatives build even more intricate nests, some of them a yard long,
like a Christmas stocking. The foliage and flowers
of the tulip tree, which frame this plate, are typical of
Audubon's interest in the landscape.

Baltimore Oriole ICTERUS BALTIMORE, *Daud.* Adult Male 1. Male two years old 2. Female 3. Toilet Tree Liriodendron tulipifera

7

Common Grackle
Quiscalus quiscula

These birds, which are lumped with
Redwings and Starlings as blackbirds, are actually members
of the same family as the Meadowlark and the
several Orioles—a diverse family, of which the grackles are probably
the least specialized. Even so, they have a keel on the
hard palate which helps them cut open acorns, which they can do by
pressing the acorns firmly with the tongue and rolling
them back and forth against the keel—no mean trick! Audubon emphasized
the nuisance these blackbirds were to the small farmer
of his day. Today—probably in large part because the countryside
is much more partitioned in the southern half of the
United States, where these birds winter—there are several large roosting
congregations of blackbirds, often in aggregations of ten
million or so. Such large numbers of birds roosting in one woodlot
night after night create many problems. In addition
to whatever other local nuisance value the grackles may have, the
great accumulation of their droppings serves to culture fungi which may,
when they blow away, cause a pneumonia-like infection.

Drawn from Nature by J.J.Audubon, F.R.S. F.L.S.

Engraved by W.H.Lizars Edin.
Retouched by R.Havell Jun.r London.

Purple Grakle or Common Crow-Blackbird
QUISCALUS VERSICOLOR, Vieill. Male 1.Female 2.   Maize or Indian Corn. Zea Mays.

159
Cardinal
Richmondena cardinalis

"How pleasing it is, when, by a
clouded sky, the woods are rendered so dark, that were it not
for an occasional glimpse of clearer light falling
between the trees, you might imagine night at hand, while you are
yet far distant from your home—how pleasing to have your ear suddenly
saluted by the well known notes of this favorite bird, assuring
you of peace around, and of the full hour that still remains for you
to pursue your walk in security! How often have I enjoyed
this pleasure, and how often, in due humbleness of hope, do I trust that
I may enjoy it again!" Audubon really felt these emotions.
Listen to his empathetic appreciation of the song of the Cardinal:
"During the love-season the song is emitted with increased emphasis by
this proud musician, who, as if aware of his powers,
swells his throat, spreads his rosy tail, droops his wings, and leans
alternately to the right and left, as if on the eve
of expiring with delight at the delicious sounds of his own voice."
Is it any wonder that Louis Agassiz Fuertes
described Audubon as "a reed bent by the
faintest breath of emotion"?

Cardinal Grosbeak.
FRINGILLA CARDINALIS, *Bonap.*
Male 1. Female 2.
Wild Almond.

Drawn from Nature by J.J. Audubon, F.R.S. F.L.S.   Engraved, Printed & Coloured by R. Havell, London 18

29
Rufous-sided Towhee
Pipilo erythrophthalmus

In Audubon's day, this saucy,
colorful bird was still called a bunting or a ground finch.
This was helpful in suggesting its relationship
to the large group of typically American birds we now call by the
grab-bag term "sparrows." The American
tendency to be very literal has given the bird its modern vernacular
name, which is a transliteration of its call-note—
"Tow-hee!" or "Che-wink!" Distinctive as the name is, it does not further
our understanding or appreciation of the Towhee,
which is but one member of a diverse group. Indeed, it has 156 species
relatives in the Americas—birds which occur from Alaska and
Labrador all the way to Argentina. The towhees are the
largest and most colorful of the group, with four species in the United
States and several more in Mexico.

PLATE XXXIX.

Towhe Bunting.

FRINGILLA ERYTHROPHTHALMA, Linn. Male, 1. Female, 2. Blackberry Rubus villosus.

PLATE

114

White-crowned Sparrow

Zonotrichia leucophrys

This species description concludes Audubon's
ornithological biography and is, besides, a testamentary statement:
"It is to the wild regions of Labrador that you must
go, kind reader, if you wish to form a personal acquaintance
with the White-crowned Sparrow. There, in every secluded
glen opening upon the boisterous Gulf of St. Lawrence, while amazed you
glance over the wilderness that extends around you,
so dreary and desolate that the blood almost congeals in your veins, you meet
with this interesting bird. In such a place when you are far
away from all that is dear to you, how cheering it is to hear the mellow
notes of a bird, that it seems as if it had been sent
expressly for the purpose of relieving your mind from the heavy melancholy
that bears it down! Thus it was with me, when, some time after
I had been landed on the dreary coast of Labrador, I for the first time heard
the song of the White-crowned Sparrow. I could
not refrain from indulging in the thought that, notwithstanding the many
difficulties attending my attempts—my mission I must call it—
to study God's works in this wild region,
I was highly favored."

PLATE CXIV

White-crowned Sparrow.

FRINGILLA LEUCOPHRYS,

Male 1. Female 2.

Summer Grape. Vitis Estivalis.

Index